G000299109

this book belongs to:

# COLOR TEST PAGE

MAKE MY
BACK
GREAT
AGAIN

Congrats
ON YOUR
NEW
BACK

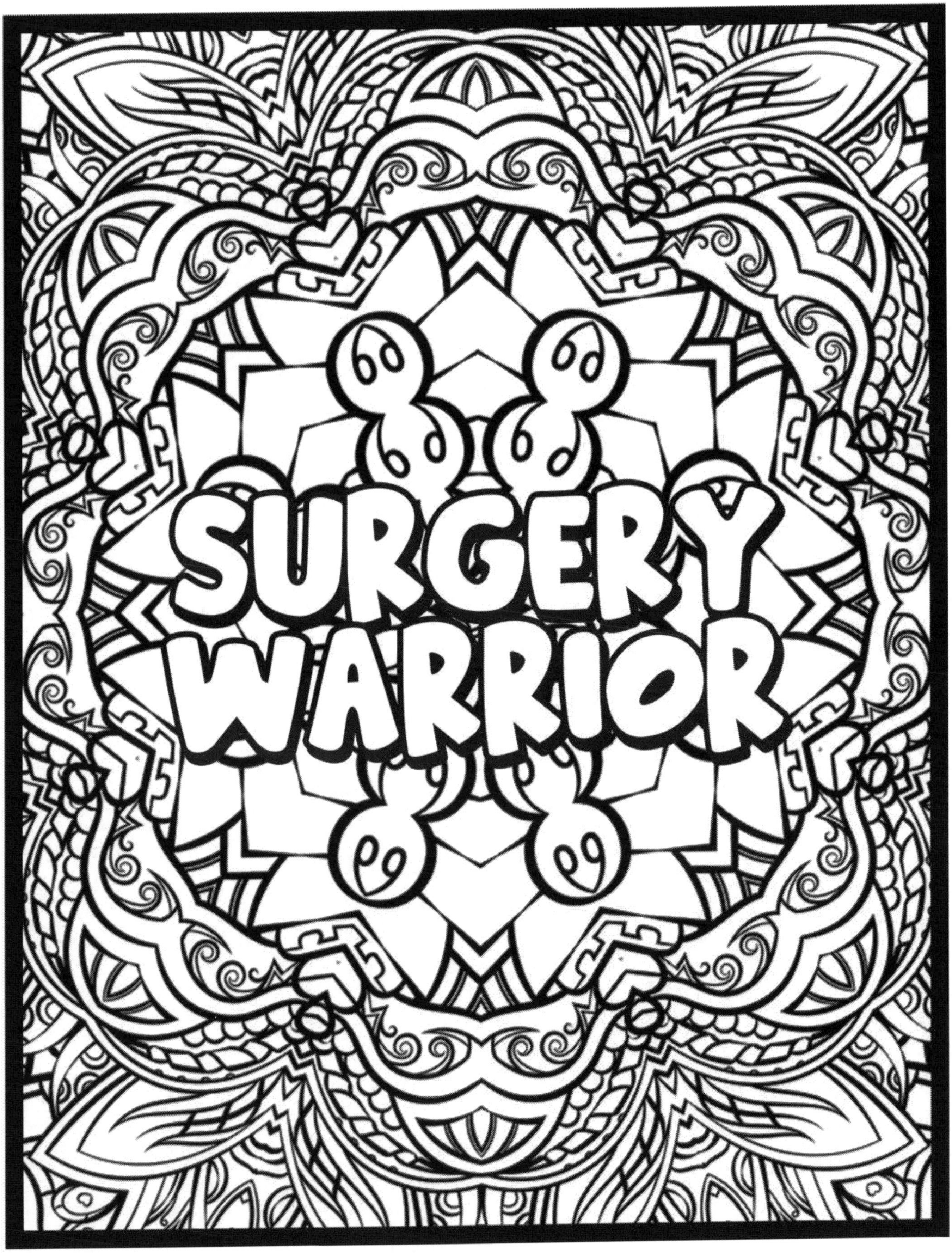
SURGERY
WARRIOR

NEW
BACK
NEW
ME

I CAN'T BE
REPLACED
BUT
MY BACK
SURE CAN

Get Well Soon

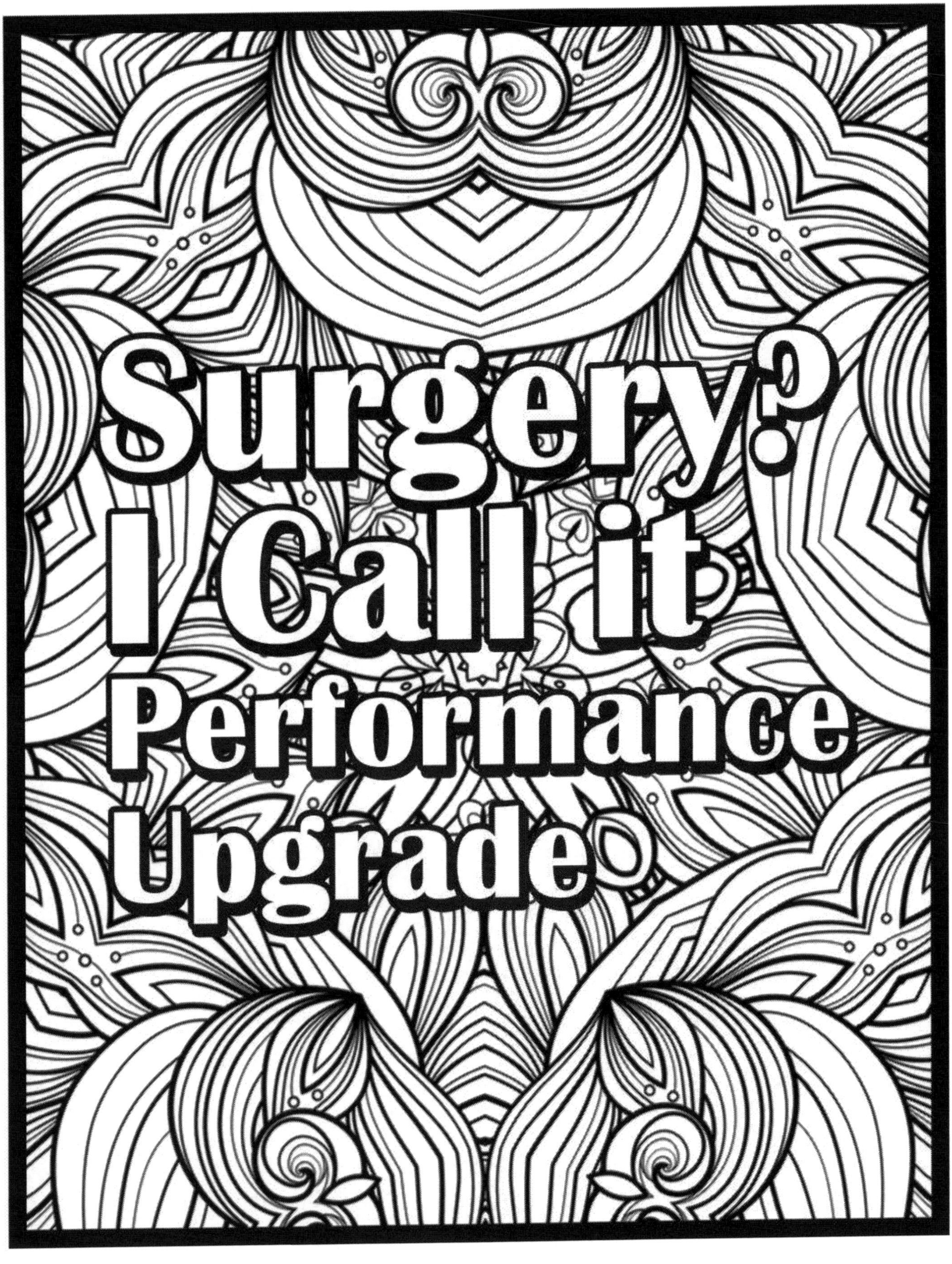
Surgery?
I Call it
Performance
Upgrade

I JUST
HAD A
Spinal
FUSION

Recovery
in
Progress

NOT EVEN
A SURGERY
CAN STOP
ME

Does my new
Back
make me look
Sexy?

I SURVIVED
BACK
SURGERY
WHAT'S YOUR
SUPERPOWER?

MY BACK
ISN'T NEW
IT'S
CERTIFIED
REFURBISHED

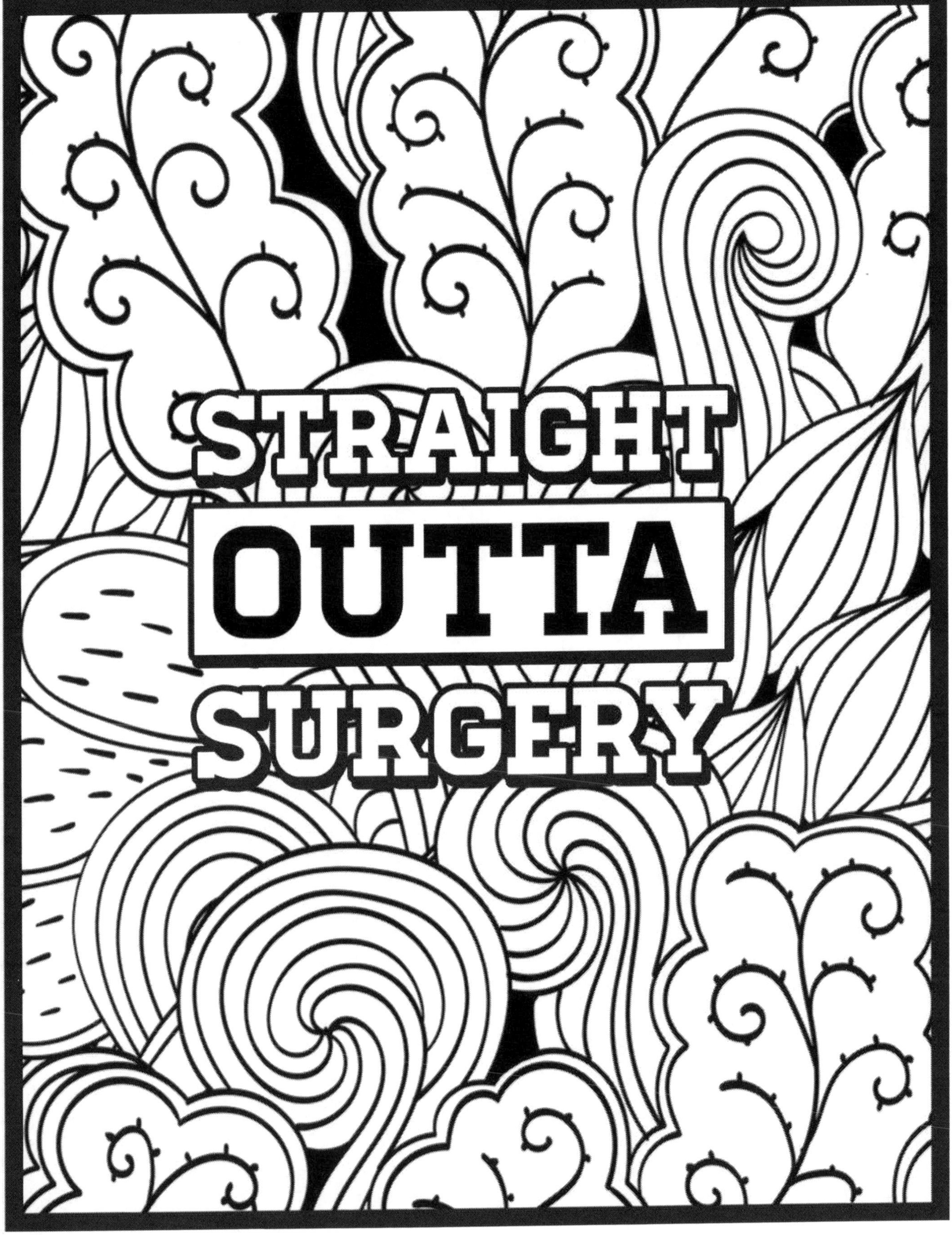
STRAIGHT
OUTTA
SURGERY

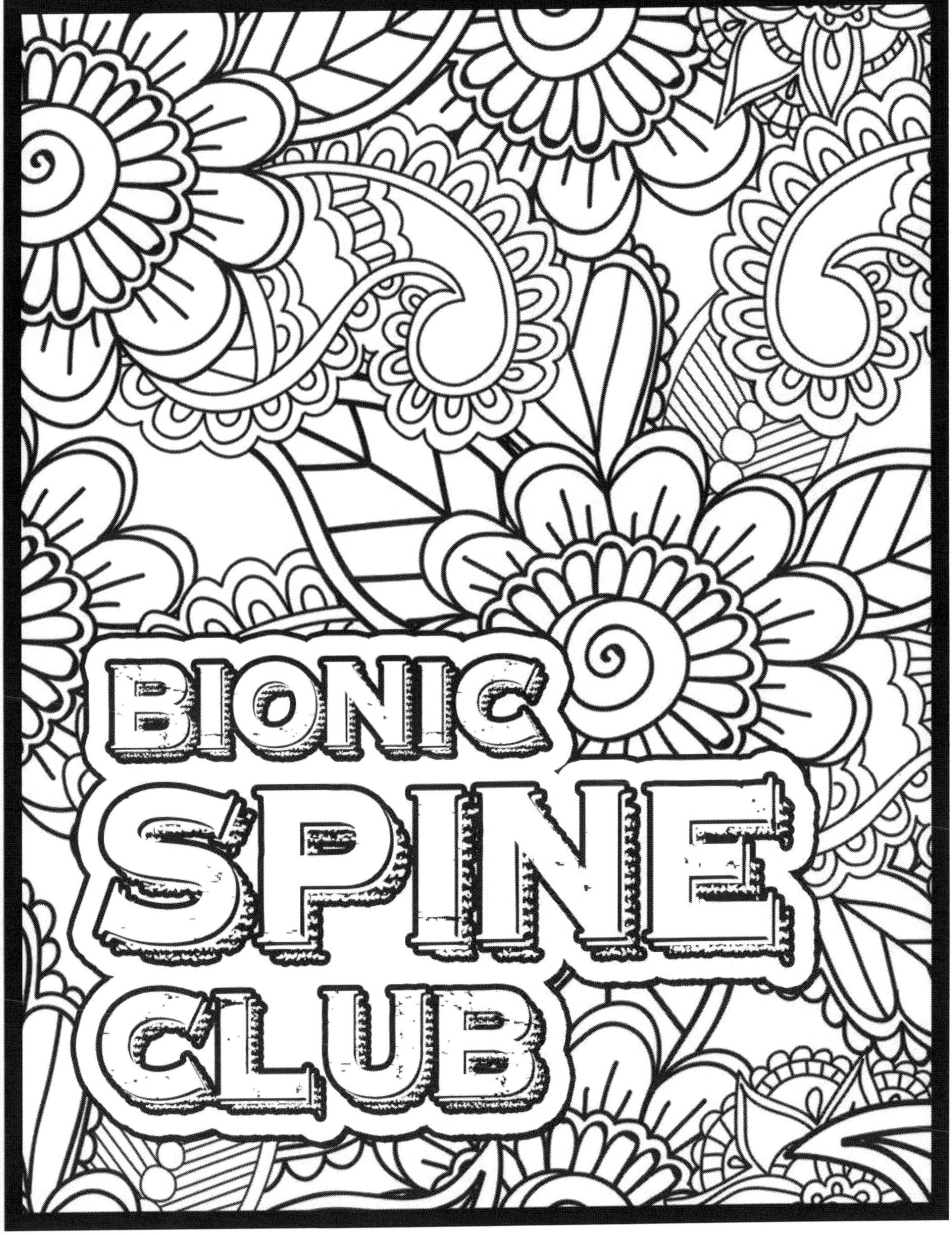
BIONIC
SPINE
CLUB

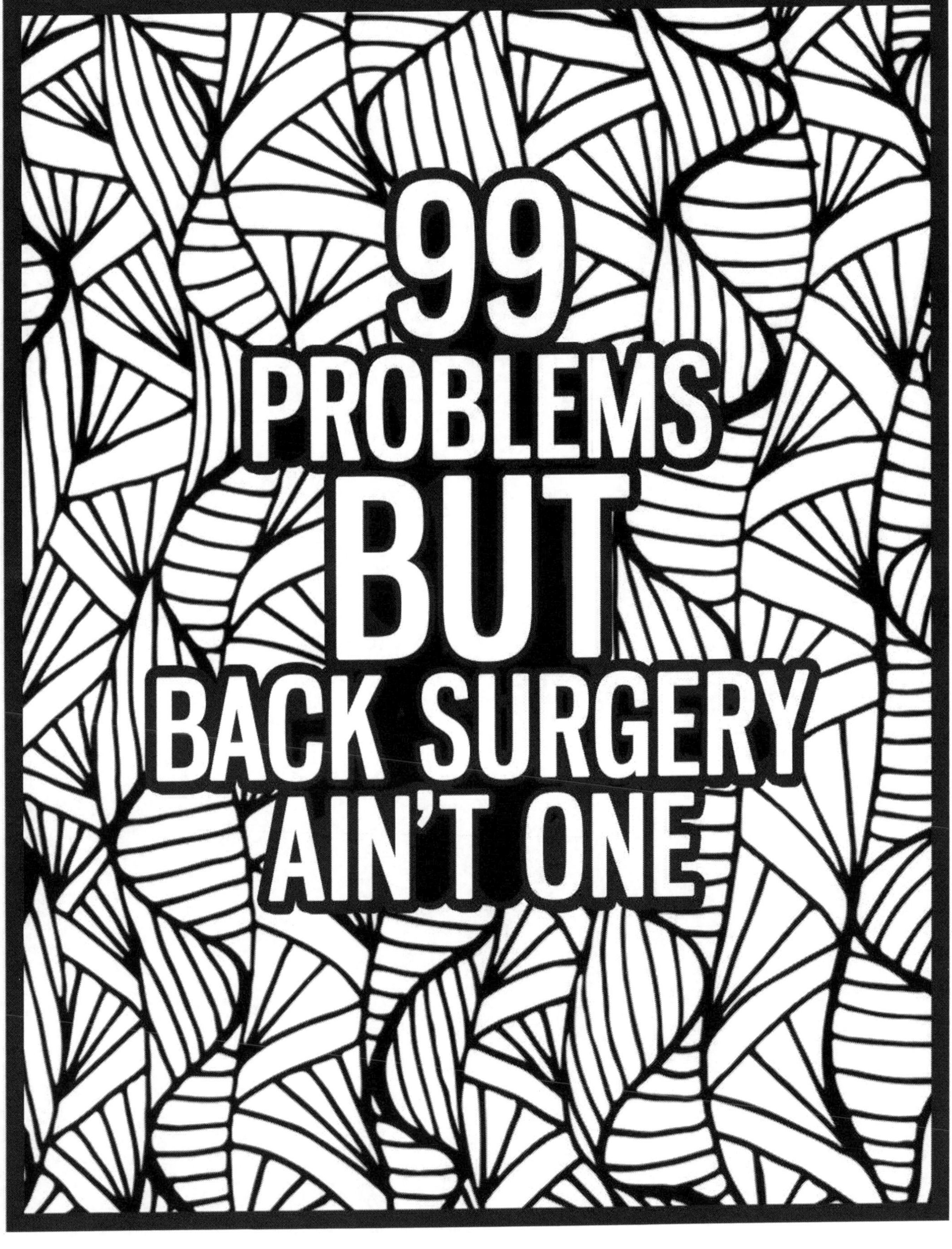
99
PROBLEMS
BUT
BACK SURGERY
AIN'T ONE

BRAND
NEW
BACK

Super
Cool
Surgery
Warrior

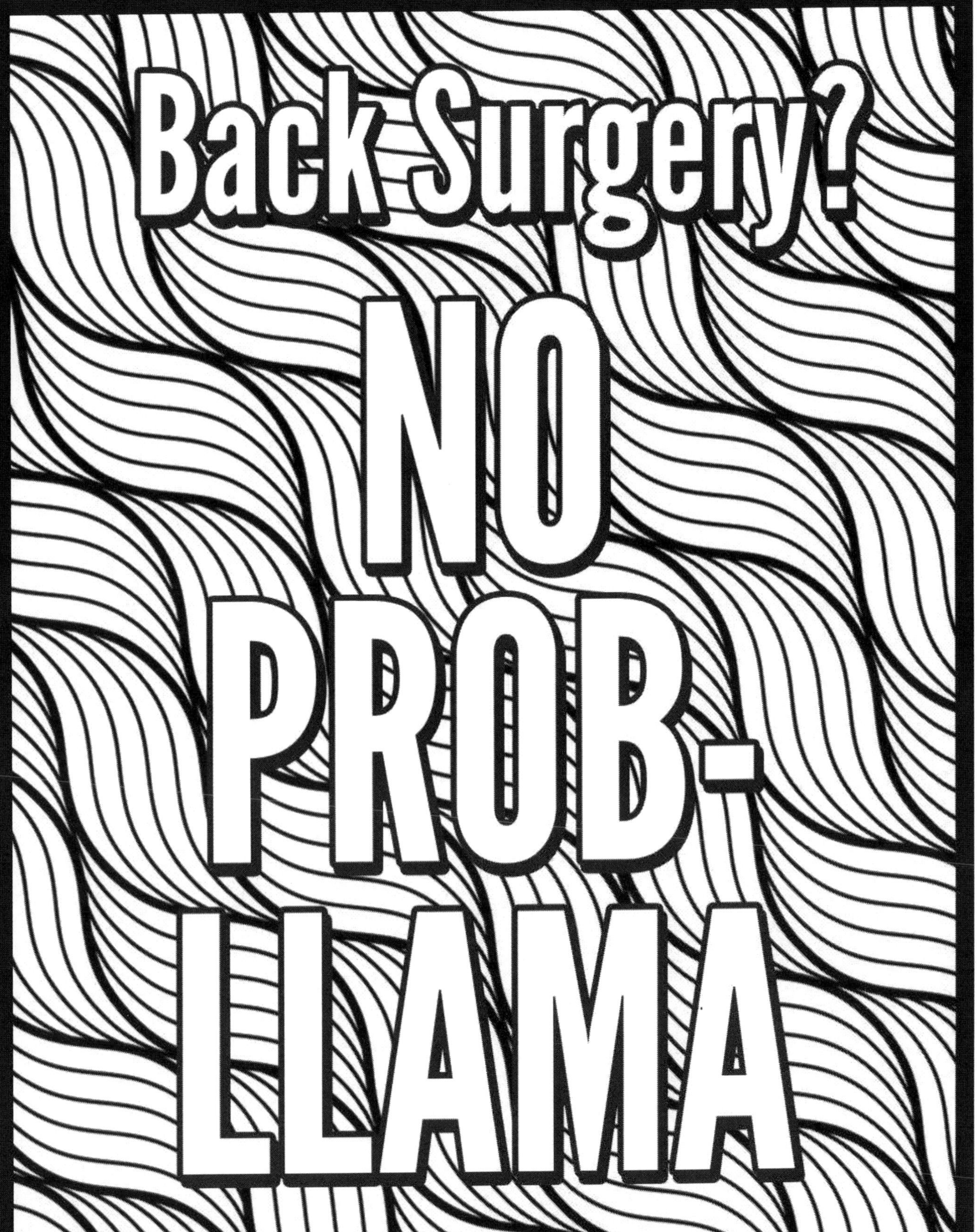
Back Surgery?
NO
PROB-
LLAMA

Recovery
Mode
On!

Printed in Great Britain
by Amazon

30762997R00026